LIGHT LEADS

THE PATH OF SOULFUL LEADERSHIP THROUGH GROWTH, PAUSE AND COMPLETION

MELITA CALLAHAN

Print ISBN: 979-8-9931632-0-8
E-book ISBN: =979-8-9931632-1-5

1st edition, October 2025

To Jo'el —

Our journey together cultivated the deepest love, the greatest lessons, and a transformation beyond measure. Through joy and through sorrow, you opened me to the wisdom of the Council of Light, and to the truth that love never ends, it only expands.

This book carries your imprint, your light,
and the eternal bond that continues to guide me.

FOREWORD

In a business world dominated by hustle culture, conversion metrics, and constant reinvention, something essential is often lost — the soul of the work. The deeper why. The quiet knowing that whispers, "There's got to be another way."

This book is that way.

Light Leads: The Path of Soulful Leadership Through Growth, Pause, and Completion is not another playbook for endless growth; it is a companion for how to discern — how to move when it's time to build, how to rest when it's time to integrate, and how to end well when a season is complete.

Light Leads offers something rare: guidance that doesn't fragment you but integrates you. It reminds us that strategy can be soulful, systems can be sacred, and a business can be an altar — not just a machine.

What makes these pages trustworthy is their honesty. This is a book that dignifies the hard parts — contraction, uncertainty, even closure — as much as it celebrates expansion. It meets this moment, when many leaders are carrying both devotion and doubt, with clear-eyed compassion.

If you are on the verge of a new offer, this book will help you lead with more heart. If you are on the verge of a hard decision, it will help you cross that threshold with integrity. Either way, you will not be asked to become more; you will be invited to return to your own light.

TABLE OF CONTENTS

LIGHT LEADS

THE PATH OF SOULFUL LEADERSHIP THROUGH GROWTH, PAUSE AND COMPLETION

INTRODUCTION

Welcome home to the field of light. You've always belonged here.

There is a quiet space between action and knowing — between striving and surrender — that many leaders miss. It is the place where soul and strategy meet. This book was born there. These 28 reflections are not steps to climb. They are invitations to listen — to your own wisdom, to the timing of your season, and to the truth of what your business is asking from you now. Sometimes that truth is to build. Sometimes it is to pause. And sometimes it is to end — not as failure, but as a sacred completion. The wisdom you will hear throughout this book is what I call the wisdom of the Field of Light. It is the living current beneath every season of business, the ground that holds us steady whether we are planting, harvesting, resting, or completing. Each chapter draws from this field — reminding us that we are never leading alone, but always within a larger rhythm of light and life. I am writing from that honesty. In this season, I am closing a business. It is humbling. It is human. And it is holy work to let something end with care. The same wisdom that once guided my growth now guides my release — to grieve, to honor what was given, and to carry forward what is still alive. This book, then, is for every season:

- When you are expanding and need alignment more than adrenaline.

- When you are tired and need rest that renews clarity.
- When you are discerning and need the courage to pivot or to close.

You don't have to force what wants to flow. You only need to remember what you already know — including the truth that completions are part of the path.

How to Use This Book in Hard Seasons

If you're uncertain: Choose one chapter and let it be your anchor for a week. Journal the prompts. Act from what emerges.

If you're contracting: Read with a highlighter for where the text gives you permission to simplify, pause, or prune.

If you're ending: Turn to the teachings on surrender, timing, and thresholds. Treat your closure as a rite of passage, not a verdict.

A Note on Stories and Examples

To protect privacy and keep the focus on the teaching, most "real-world reflections" are illustrative composites — representative scenarios drawn from patterns I've seen. When a story is my own, I name it as such.

What You Can Expect

- Spiritual depth without bypassing reality.
- Practical practices that honor both the spiritual and the structural.
- Language that honors beginnings, middles, and endings with equal dignity.

Business isn't separate from spirit. Your vision is sacred. Your work — whether it is growing, resting, or completing, is a field of possibility. The light never leaves you. It simply waits for your return.

Welcome to the light.

CHAPTER 1:
The Field of Vision

Vision is not just what you want to create, but what you are called to hold. It is the compass that orients you when the market shifts, when your energy rises and falls, and when uncertainty clouds the path ahead.

A true vision is both anchor and horizon. It grounds you in what matters most while pulling you toward the future that wants to emerge. Without vision, business can quickly become reactive, driven by urgency or metrics that don't reflect the soul of your work. With vision, even hard decisions — pruning an offer, slowing growth, or closing with dignity — find their place in a larger unfolding.

Beyond Strategy, Into Soul

Too often, we treat vision as a slogan, a branding exercise, or a five-year plan. But soul-aligned vision is deeper. It is not crafted only from logic; it is remembered. It emerges from the heart and carries threads from your lineage, your experiences, and your highest self.

Your vision is not static. Like the seasons, it evolves. Sometimes it invites expansion. Sometimes it asks for a pause. And sometimes it becomes a lantern guiding you through sacred completion.

Real-World Reflection

Consider Elena, a creative studio founder, who arrived at a crossroad. On paper, her business was thriving — profitable projects, recognizable clients, steady growth. But inside, she felt hollow. Each project became work-for-hire rather than the expression of her creative calling.

Instead of pushing harder, Elena paused. She wrote a manifesto for her work, naming what her business stood for and what no longer fit. In the process, she pruned offerings that drained her and allowed space for something more aligned to emerge. Her vision didn't just lead her forward — it clarified what was complete.

The wisdom of the field reminds us:

- Vision is not performance; it is presence.

- You don't have to manufacture clarity; you need only remember what your heart already knows.

- Vision dignifies endings as much as beginnings — every closure is also a completion within the whole.

When you orient by this kind of vision, your business becomes more than a series of goals. It becomes a living field of possibility.

Practice: The Living Manifesto

Write a one-page manifesto for your business as if it were a living being. Ask:

- What does it stand for?

- What season is it in - growth, pause, or completion?

- What is it asking you to release?

Read it aloud. Notice where your body feels energy rise, and where it contracts. These are clues to your true direction.

Reflection Questions

- What is my vision asking of me now?

- Where is my vision misaligned with my current offerings?

- What part of my vision might be complete — making space for what wants to be born?

CHAPTER 2:
Alignment

Alignment is the invisible current that makes everything flow with less effort. When your actions, offers, and values resonate with one another, energy is multiplied. When they conflict, even small tasks become heavy. Alignment is not about perfection or constant harmony — it is about noticing when something is off and courageously returning to truth.

The Cost of Misalignment

Many businesses falter not because of poor strategy, but because of hidden misalignment. You may be chasing numbers that don't reflect your real goals, saying yes when your body is screaming no, or designing systems that look impressive but drain your spirit.

Alignment is not about doing more; often it means letting go. True alignment dignifies endings as much as beginnings. It allows you to prune what no longer belongs so that what remains can flourish.

Real World Reflection

Take Simone, a systems strategist, who once poured energy into elaborate funnels. They dazzled on paper but felt hollow in practice.

She noticed that she spent more energy maintaining the machine than serving clients. Her schedule was full, but her soul was absent.

Alignment invited her to simplify. She stripped away what no longer resonated and redesigned her offers around clarity and ease. This wasn't just about efficiency — it was about integrity. In saying no to complexity, she made space for more presence, more service, and more joy.

From the field we learn:

- Alignment is resonance. When you act from alignment, you stop pushing and start flowing.

- Misalignment is not a failure — it is feedback, showing you what is ready to be released.

- Alignment is not static. What fits one season may not belong in the next. The soul always makes space for renewal.

This teaching frees you from clinging to what once worked but now weighs you down. Alignment allows you to pivot, to pause, or to end — and trust that these are not losses, but pathways to truth.

Practice: The Alignment Audit

Take out your weekly calendar. Map your activities against your deepest values.

- Circle what feels alive, nourishing, and true.
- Cross out what feels draining, heavy, or false.

For the places of dissonance, ask: Does this need a shift, a pause, or a completion?

Treat this as a living ritual, not a one-time exercise. Alignment is dynamic; it asks for ongoing attention.

Reflection Questions

- Where in my business am I out of alignment?

- What am I doing only because I think I "should"?

- What would alignment look like if I honored endings as much as beginnings?

CHAPTER 3:
Authority

True authority does not come from titles, credentials, or external validation. It arises from embodied integrity — when your words, actions, and values align. Authority is not about proving; it is about presence.

When you stand in your own authority, people sense it. Not because you are the loudest in the room, but because your voice carries the weight of truth. Authority requires both courage and humility: the courage to stand firm in your knowing, and the humility to admit when something no longer belongs.

Beyond Performing Authority

In today's business world, authority is often confused with performance. You may feel pressure to appear certain, polished, and endlessly productive. But real authority is not about holding it all together at any cost — it is about knowing when to pause, when to slow down, and even when to end.

Authority deepens when you stop performing and start embodying. It is strengthened not by doing more, but by leading with clarity, even if that clarity asks you to release what no longer feels true.

Real-World Reflection

Leila, a startup advisor, discovered this firsthand. Her launch strategies succeeded on paper, but each one left her exhausted. She realized her authority had become performative — proving she could deliver at any cost.

When she began reclaiming her voice, she allowed herself to choose a slower pace. She rested between launches. She ended programs that no longer felt alive. Paradoxically, her authority grew stronger. Clients trusted her more, not because she did more, but because she stood in deeper conviction.

The field reminds us:

- Authority is not bestowed — it is embodied.
- Pretending to know drains energy; admitting the truth builds trust.
- Sometimes the most powerful act of authority is to say: "This is complete."

Authority is not control. It is alignment. It is the steady presence that communicates: "I trust myself enough to lead from truth, not from fear."

Practice: The Voice of Authority

Record yourself speaking about your work for three minutes without notes. Then listen back:

- Note the words and phrases that feel alive, authentic, and magnetic.
- Notice where your energy drops — these are places that may be misaligned or asking to be released.

This practice reveals the difference between what you perform and what you embody.

Reflection Questions

- What gives me the deepest sense of authority in my work?

- Where am I performing authority instead of embodying it?

- What would it look like to end something that undermines my authority?

CHAPTER 4:
Timing

Every vision has its season. Forcing something before its time creates strain; delaying too long lets momentum dissolve. Sacred timing is not about speed — it is about attunement. It is learning to move with the cycles of energy, market, and spirit, rather than against them.

The Myth of Urgency

In the culture of business, urgency is glorified. We are told to act quickly, to seize every opportunity, to fear falling behind. But urgency is not always alignment. Sometimes what appears like momentum is simply pressure, and what feels like delay is actually gestation.

Sacred timing asks us to pause long enough to discern: is this opportunity ripe, or am I trying to force fruit from a seed not yet sprouted?

Real World Reflection

Daniel, a leadership coach, felt this tension. Investors urged him to scale quickly, expand programs, and capture market share. On paper, it seemed like the smart move. But inwardly, he felt scattered and unstable. His systems weren't ready.

By pausing, Daniel discerned that what was needed wasn't acceleration but consolidation. He slowed down, strengthened his foundation, and ended scattered projects that were diffusing his energy. In honoring timing, he discovered that sometimes the wisest choice is not to grow faster, but to root deeper.

The field offers us this wisdom:

Right timing is a form of trust. You don't need to force what is meant for you.

Delay is not denial; sometimes it is protection.

Endings are also timing — not everything is meant to be carried forward.

When you align with sacred timing, you discover that your work expands with less strain. Opportunities arrive when you are ready to hold them, not when fear tells you to rush.

Practice: The Timing Triage

Each month, list three opportunities, projects, or decisions you feel pressure to pursue. Then:

- Circle the one that feels ripe now.
- Cross out the one that feels premature or forced.
- Place the third on a "someday" list to revisit later.

This practice helps you discern between urgency and true readiness.

Reflection Questions

- What am I trying to force before it's season?
- What is ripe and ready now?
- What is asking to be delayed, or even completed?

CHAPTER 5:

The Sacred No

Saying no is not rejection — it is devotion. Every "no" protects your energy, clarifies your "yes," and creates space for what is truly aligned to emerge.

In business, it is easy to equate worth with how much you can hold. Every request answered, every opportunity pursued, every invitation accepted. But overcommitting fractures integrity and depletes vitality. The Sacred No reminds us that boundaries are holy, and that endings, too, can be acts of leadership.

The Power of Refusal

Each "no" is a threshold. It says: I will no longer abandon myself for approval. I will no longer dilute my energy to maintain appearances. I will no longer sacrifice my devotion to sustain what is already complete.

Your no is not selfish; it is sacred. It frees you from what is false so that you can offer yourself fully to what is true.

Real-World Reflection

Jonah, a product designer, once said yes to nearly every request. His calendar was overflowing, his creativity diluted, his joy dimmed. It wasn't until he began saying no — declining projects, limiting

His "no" became a doorway. It wasn't just about conserving time; it was about reclaiming presence. Each no became a rite of passage — a recognition that something had served its purpose and could now be released.

The Field of Light whispers:

- No is not absence; it is alignment.
- Each no makes room for a deeper yes.
- Sometimes, no is the most honest way to honor completion.

The Sacred No is not resistance but reverence. It honors what matters most, even if it disappoints others.

Practice: The Devotional No

For one week, track every request that comes your way — emails, collaborations, invitations, even internal impulses. Each day, choose at least one thing to decline, gently but firmly.

Notice how your body responds. Do you feel lighter, clearer, more spacious? Let each no become a practice of devotion — to your work, your energy, and your truth.

Reflection Questions

- Where am I called to say no right now?
- What ends when I decline, and what space opens up?
- How could a "no" be an act of completion rather than resistance?

CHAPTER 6:
Devotion

Devotion is the current that sustains you when excitement fades. It is the deeper why beneath every task, the steady flame that keeps you aligned when outcomes fluctuate.

Discipline can push you forward, but devotion pulls you deeper. Discipline says do it anyway; devotion says return because you love it. When rooted in devotion, your business ceases to be a machine you must fuel and becomes a practice you get to tend.

Devotion vs. Depletion

It is easy to confuse devotion with overwork. You may believe that working longer hours, being always available, or never taking a break is a sign of commitment. But true devotion doesn't drain; it replenishes.

Real-World Reflection

Maya, a consultant, built her reputation on being available 24/7. Emails at midnight, calls at all hours, weekends consumed by work. She believed this was devotion — until exhaustion told another story. Only when she set boundaries, paused, and released contracts that eroded her energy did she realize: devotion is not about doing everything. It is about caring for what matters most.

The field reminds us:

- Devotion dignifies both beginnings and endings.

- Devotion is not measured by hours spent, but by presence offered.

- Devotion asks for rest, boundaries, and ritual — not relentless output.

When you bring devotion into your leadership, even mundane tasks can become sacred. Sending an email, preparing a proposal, closing your books — all become offerings, not obligations.

Practice: Letters of Love and Release

Write a love letter to your work — naming what you cherish, what still lights you up, and what you feel called to sustain.

Then, write a farewell letter to any part of your business that no longer aligns. Thank it for what it gave you, and release it with grace.

Both letters are acts of devotion. One honors what you are carrying forward; the other dignifies what is complete.

Reflection Questions

- What am I most devoted to now?

- Where has devotion turned into exhaustion?

- What would devotion look like if I honored rest and endings as much as beginnings?

CHAPTER 7:
Rhythm of Launches

Launching is not about endless momentum — it is about rhythm. Just as the earth moves through cycles of planting, blossoming, harvest, and rest, your business thrives when it honors natural seasons. Every launch requires preparation, offering, integration, and renewal. Without this rhythm, what once felt exciting quickly turns into exhaustion.

Beyond the Hustle of Back-to-Back Launches

In the culture of online business, launches are often stacked one after another. The mantra is more: more offers, more visibility, more growth. But without rest, each launch draws from a depleted well, leaving both leader and community fatigued.

Rhythm asks you to step back, to see the wider arc: not every season is harvest. Sometimes the soil needs to lie fallow. Sometimes an offer has completed its cycle and is asking for closure rather than repetition.

Real-World Reflection

Leila, a startup advisor, once built her business on successful launches. On the surface, everything worked — sign-ups filled, revenue grew. Yet each launch left her emptier, as though her energy was being wrung dry.

Her turning point came when she allowed rhythm to guide her. She began spacing launches to include intentional pauses. She restructured her calendar to include integration time. And when an offer no longer felt alive, she ended it rather than repeating out of habit. Her results did not diminish — they deepened. Clients trusted her more because she led from sustainability, not from urgency.

The field whispers:

- Launches are not isolated events; they are part of a living cycle.

- Rest is not absence but preparation. Integration is as sacred as initiation.

- Endings are natural — some offerings complete their season, making space for new growth.

When you align with rhythm, launches become less about pressure and more about participation in a cycle bigger than yourself.

Practice: Cycle Mapping

Draw a simple wheel of the year, divided into four seasons. Place your launches on this wheel. Then, mark:

- Which season is for planting (visioning, pre-launch groundwork)?

- Which is for blossoming (the active launch)?

- Which is for harvest (serving, delivering, receiving the fruits)?

- Which is for rest (integration, reflection, renewal)?

Notice: Are you honoring each phase, or skipping straight from planting to planting, never allowing the soil to restore?

Reflection Questions

- What is my natural rhythm of creating and resting?

- Which offerings are ready for another launch, and which are complete?

- How can I honor the fallow season as much as the harvest?

CHAPTER 8::
Integrity

Integrity is the alignment between what you promise and what you deliver, what you value and how you act. It is the wholeness of your leadership. Without integrity, even the most brilliant vision loses its power; with it, even difficult seasons can be walked with dignity.

The Wholeness of Leadership

Integrity is not about perfection. It is about congruence. When your words and actions match, when your choices reflect your values, you stand whole. When they do not, energy leaks. Clients sense it, teams feel it, and you carry the quiet weight of misalignment.

Sometimes integrity asks you to keep going. Sometimes it asks you to pause. And sometimes it asks you to end — not as failure, but as fidelity to truth.

Real-World Reflection

Rafael, a nonprofit founder, carried his mission with passion but also with a burden. For years, he pushed beyond his limits, single-handedly sustaining programs that no longer had resources or resonance. Donors admired the outcomes, but inside, the organization frayed.

Integrity called him not to push harder, but to realign. He shared responsibility with his team, paused projects that had lost support, and allowed some programs to close with grace. Far from diminishing his leadership, these acts deepened trust. His community saw a leader willing to embody wholeness rather than performance.

The field teaches:

- Integrity is spacious — it makes room for truth, even when truth disrupts plans.

- To remain whole, you must release what fragments you.

- Integrity is not rigidity; it is the courage to adapt while staying faithful to your essence.

This means integrity can look like scaling back, restructuring, or completing an offer. It can also look like admitting, "This is no longer sustainable," and choosing presence over performance.

Practice: The Integrity Inventory

Write a list of all your current commitments — clients, projects, collaborations, and internal goals. For each, ask:

- Does this still feel true?

- Does this reflect my deepest values?

- If not, what would integrity call me to do — pause, shift, or complete?

Let this audit become a regular rhythm. Each realignment restores wholeness.

Reflection Questions

- Where am I living in integrity?

- Where have I drifted from what I most value?

- What commitments might need to be released to restore wholeness?

CHAPTER 9:
Courage

Courage is not the absence of fear — it is the willingness to move with truth even when fear lingers. In business, courage takes many forms: beginning a new venture, speaking an unpopular truth, saying no to what no longer serves, or ending something beloved but complete.

Courage Beyond Bold Moves

We often imagine courage as dramatic — taking the leap, launching big, standing tall. But courage is equally present in quiet moments: admitting what isn't working, trusting an inner nudge, or choosing rest over relentless hustle.

Courage is less about heroics and more about honesty. It asks you to listen for the truth beneath your fear — and then act from that place, no matter how small the step.

Real-World Reflection

Leena, a marketing director, exemplified this truth. She worked in a lucrative, high-profile role that looked enviable from the outside. But inside, she felt hollow. Each campaign drained her; each meeting pulled her further from her values.

The courageous act was not another bold project. It was resigning. Choosing to walk away from what no longer fit, even without a clear map for what comes next. Her decision was frightening but also liberating. In choosing completion, she made space for work that felt alive again.

The field reminds us:

- Courage is not always about expansion; sometimes it is about release.

- Fear is not the enemy — it is a signal pointing you toward your growing edge.

- Every ending that requires courage is also an initiation into new wholeness.

To lead with courage is to trust that truth itself is enough — even when outcomes are uncertain.

Practice: Naming the Fear, Honoring the Truth

Each week, name one thing you are afraid to admit about your business or leadership. Please write it down. Share it, if you can, with a trusted peer or mentor.

Then ask:

- What truth is this fear protecting?

- What would courage look like here — to act, to wait, or to end?

By naming fear and uncovering the truth beneath it, you invite courage to walk with you.

Reflection Questions

- Where is fear holding me back from the truth?

- What action would courage take now?

- What would it mean to complete something courageously?

CHAPTER 10:
Rest

Rest is not the opposite of work — it is part of the work. Every cycle of creation requires cycles of renewal. Without rest, momentum collapses, clarity dulls, and even the most inspired vision begins to wither.

The Sacred Pause

In a culture that glorifies hustle, rest is often mistaken for laziness or weakness. But in truth, rest is a sacred rebellion. It is the choice to trust that your value does not come from constant output, and that integration is as essential as initiation.

Rest restores perspective. It allows your nervous system to catch up with your ambition. It clears the fog of overwork and reconnects you with why you began. Far from slowing you down, rest returns you to alignment.

Real World Reflection

For much of my life, I did not allow myself true, deep rest. I paused only long enough to recover before pushing back into work, family responsibilities, or business demands. My worth was tied to doing — to being a contributor, a provider, a constant engine of productivity.

It wasn't until my cancer journey that I was forced into an extended season of rest. Treatment and surgical recovery left me no choice but to stop. At first, it was excruciating — not only physically, but mentally. Who was I if I wasn't producing? How could I matter if I wasn't carrying my company, my family, or my household? That season challenged my very identity as a doer. And yet, it also gave me the deepest initiation into rest as sacred work. I discovered that value doesn't come only from output. Presence, healing, and simply being held by life became their own form of contribution. It is a lesson I am still integrating. Rest isn't easy for me, but I now see it as essential — not just for recovery, but for renewal, clarity, and wholeness.

The field reminds us:

- Rest is not an afterthought; it is part of devotion.
- Renewal is not indulgence; it is responsibility.

Endings often create the deepest rest — releasing what drains you allows new vitality to rise.

To lead with light is to remember that rest is not optional. It is a form of leadership.

Practice: Rhythms of Renewal

Schedule three kinds of rest into your life and business:

- Daily pauses — short breaks that reset your energy.
- Weekly renewal — longer moments of restoration, like a day of rest, nature walks, or play.
- Seasonal retreats — intentional times of stepping away from your business to listen, restore, and reconnect.

Protect these spaces as fiercely as you protect deadlines. They are not luxuries — they are leadership practices.

Reflection Questions

- What kind of rest do I resist most?
- Where does my business need a pause?
- What might need to end so that true rest is possible?

CHAPTER 11:
Listening

Listening is the foundation of wisdom. It is more than hearing words
— it is opening yourself to the guidance within and around you. In
business, listening allows you to discern truth beneath noise, to hear
the needs of clients and teams, and to honor the quiet wisdom of your
own soul.

Beyond Surface Hearing

Most leaders are trained to respond quickly, to solve problems, to fill
silence with answers. But real listening requires stillness. It asks us to
hear not only what is said but what is left unspoken — the hesitations,
the pauses, the emotions beneath the words.

Listening is also attunement to timing: when to move, when to pause,
and when a season of work or partnership is complete.

Real World Reflection

Omar, a facilitator, noticed he often rushed to reassure clients when
silence arose. He feared awkwardness, so he filled the space with
advice. But when he practiced pausing — waiting a full minute before

speaking — something shifted. Clients began sharing deeper truths. He realized that by softening his need to fix, he created space for wisdom to emerge.

This practice transformed his leadership. Listening became not just a technique, but a way of honoring others and himself.

The field reminds us:

- Silence is not emptiness — it is an invitation.

- When you resist listening, you resist growth.

- Sometimes the most important message is the one that arrives when you stop speaking.

Listening is not passive. It is an active presence. It requires humility to be with what is, without rushing to change it.

Practice: The One-Question Silence

In your next conversation — with a client, a colleague, or yourself — ask a single open-ended question. Then remain silent for at least one full minute. Resist the urge to fill the space. Notice what arises.

This practice cultivates patience, presence, and trust that wisdom does not need to be forced — it will surface in its own time.

Reflection Questions

- Where am I avoiding listening because it feels uncomfortable?

- What is my business asking me to hear right now?

- What pauses or completions are being whispered to me that I ignore?

CHAPTER 12

Boundaries as Devotion

Boundaries are not walls. They are sacred lines that protect what you love. Without them, devotion becomes depletion. With them, your energy, creativity, and clarity are preserved for what matters most.

The Sacred Role of Boundaries

In business, boundaries are often misunderstood. Some view them as restrictive or unkind. But boundaries are not about keeping others out — they are about keeping you in. They protect the integrity of your work and the sustainability of your leadership.

Without boundaries, exhaustion sets in. Commitments blur. The very work you once loved begins to feel heavy. Boundaries, then, are not acts of rejection. They are acts of reverence.

Real-World Reflection

Maya, a consultant, built her reputation on always being available. Emails answered at midnight, weekend calls, urgent texts — her devotion blurred into overextension. Inevitably, she burned out.

Only when she set clear boundaries did she rediscover her devotion. She created office hours, honored days off, and chose not to take on clients who disrespected her limits. Far from losing clients, she attracted ones who valued her clarity. Her business didn't shrink; it strengthened. The field reminds us:

- Boundaries are not barriers; they are bridges to sustainability.

- Saying no is often the truest form of devotion.

- Healthy boundaries create space for deeper love, presence, and longevity in your work.

Boundaries are how devotion stays alive — not by doing everything, but by tending what is truly yours to hold.

Practice: The Boundary Audit

This month, choose one area of your business to bring into alignment. Ask:

- Where do I feel resentment building?

- Where am I giving more than I wish to give?

- What boundary would restore devotion here?

Then set one new boundary — whether it's response times, meeting limits, or project scope. Communicate it clearly and honor it consistently.

Reflection Questions

- Where does my lack of boundaries erode my devotion?

- What new boundary would nourish me most?

- What might need to end if I am to stay true to myself?

CHAPTER 13:
Trust

Trust is the steady ground of leadership. It is built not in grand gestures, but in consistency, honesty, and presence. Trust cannot be forced or faked; it grows slowly, through alignment between word and deed.

The Slow Work of Trust

In a business culture obsessed with quick wins, trust asks for patience. One promise kept at a time. One truth spoken when it would have been easier to exaggerate. One moment of presence instead of distraction.

Trust is fragile when built on performance. But when built on integrity, it endures. It sustains you in seasons of uncertainty and strengthens your relationships with clients, collaborators, and yourself.

Real-World Reflection

Lila, a coach, felt pressure to overpromise results. The temptation was strong — bold claims sold faster. Instead, she chose honesty, even when it cost her a client. She told the truth about what she could offer and what she could not.

Over time, her trust deepened. People came to her not because she promised everything, but because they knew she would deliver what she did promise — and admit when something had reached completion. Trust became her true brand, more magnetic than any marketing campaign.

The field reminds us:

- Trust is not built on outcomes but on presence

- Honesty is trust's most powerful seed.

Sometimes trust is strengthened by completion — by ending what no longer serves, rather than pretending it still does.

To trust yourself is to believe in your own alignment more than external approval. To build trust with others is to show them that your yes means yes, and your no means no.

Practice: The Trust Ledger

Create a journal or document where you list evidence of trust in your business. Record moments when:

- A client came easily without forcing.

- A pivot worked even when logic doubted it.

- A synchronicity opened doors. A promise was honored, even in difficulty.

When doubt creeps in, return to this ledger. Let it remind you that trust has already carried you this far — and will continue to do so.

Reflection Questions

- Where am I tempted to exaggerate or overcommit?

- What does trustworthy leadership look like for me right now?

- Where might trust be strengthened by closure instead of continuation?

CHAPTER 14:
Power

Power is the ability to act in alignment with truth. It is not domination, but stewardship — the capacity to direct energy wisely, to know when to move, and to know when to stop.

Redefining Power

Many leaders mistake power for control, speed, or force. But true power is quieter. It flows when your choices match your values. It strengthens when you honor your limits. It multiplies when you empower others rather than hoarding authority for yourself.

Sometimes the most powerful act is to begin. Other times, the most powerful act is to conclude.

Real World Reflection

Angela, the owner of a boutique wellness shop, struggled with dwindling revenue. She felt pressure to add more products, host constant events, and extend her hours to stay competitive. The result? Exhaustion, debt, and a fraying sense of joy.

Her turning point came when she redefined power. Instead of expanding further, she paused. She discontinued slow moving inventory, reduced hours to protect her energy, and chose to invest in fewer but more aligned offerings — locally made products that resonated with her community.

By reclaiming her power, Angela discovered that less was more. Sales steadied, her overhead decreased, and her customers began to see her shop not as just another store, but as a curated sanctuary. Her willingness to stop doing what wasn't working was an act of power — one that saved both her business and her spirit.

The field reminds us:

- Power is not about forcing outcomes — it is about aligned action.
- Withholding truth drains power; speaking it restores it.
- Sometimes the most powerful act is to stop — to end, to pause, to redirect.
- Power thrives in clarity. It is strongest when guided by integrity and love.

Practice: Power Reclaimed

List three areas in your business or leadership where you feel most drained. For each, ask:

- What truth have I been avoiding here?
- What decision would release energy back to me?
- Is it time to act, to delegate, or to end?

Choose one small but powerful action this week — not to prove your strength, but to align your energy.

Reflection Questions

- Where am I giving away my power?

- How does aligned power want to move through me now?

- Where might the most powerful act be to stop, rather than to continue?

- What decision would release energy back to me?

CHAPTER 15:
Community

Community is both a resource and a responsibility. True leadership is never solitary; it is shared. To build with light means to recognize that belonging is as vital for you as it is for those you serve.

The Myth of Going Alone

Entrepreneurship and leadership often glorify independence. We admire the lone visionary, the self-made story, the myth of carrying it all yourself. But isolation is not a strength. Without community, creativity dims, resilience falters, and vision becomes heavy.

Community is not just about who you serve; it is also about who holds you. It is the web of support that steadies you in growth, anchors you in endings, and reminds you that you are not alone in the in-between.

Real World Reflection

Ana, a founder of a small coworking space, tried to carry her vision alone. She believed asking for help would burden others, so she worked late nights, managed all the logistics, and shouldered every financial risk herself. Eventually, she collapsed under the weight.

When she finally opened her circle — inviting members to co-create events, asking friends to help brainstorm funding, and sharing honestly about the challenges — something shifted. Her community didn't resent her vulnerability; they respected it. They wanted to contribute. The coworking space became more than her business — it became their shared home.

Ana's leadership deepened not because she carried more, but because she allowed herself to be carried, too.

The field reminds us:

- Community holds us not only in beginnings, but also in endings.
- Belonging is reciprocal — you give, but you must also receive.
- Vulnerability is not weakness; it is the doorway to authentic connection.

When you lead from community, your work becomes a shared field of light, stronger than anything you could sustain alone.

Practice: Three Honest Shares

Reach out to three peers, colleagues, or members of your circle. Share one honest update with each — not just successes, but struggles. Notice who can hold you with care. Let this become a doorway into deeper belonging.

Reflection Questions

- Where am I isolating instead of leaning into community?
- What support am I resisting?
- Who could help me honor a pause or an ending with dignity?

CHAPTER 16:
Creativity

Creativity is the life-force of business. It is what renews what feels stale and brings surprise where systems grow rigid. Without creativity, your work becomes mechanical. With creativity, it becomes alive.

Making Space for Emergence

Creativity cannot be forced. It arrives when there is room for it to breathe. Often, we suffocate creativity by overscheduling, over-planning, or clinging to what worked in the past. True creativity flows in cycles — inspiration, expression, integration, rest.

To lead creatively is to honor these rhythms. Sometimes it means beginning something new. Sometimes it means retiring what no longer serves, so fresh inspiration can emerge.

Real-World Reflection

Kai, a designer, realized he was repeating the same templates and styles because they were safe and familiar. His work looked polished, but it no longer carried spark. Clients sensed the difference.

He began experimenting again — not by adding more, but by subtracting. He retired outdated packages, paused projects that drained him, and gave himself time to play without outcome. In releasing what no longer fit, his creativity reawakened. New ideas surfaced. His clients felt the vitality return, and his business began to grow in a way that felt alive again.

The field reminds us:

- Creativity thrives on space — endings create room for beginnings.
- Innovation is not just about addition; it is also about subtraction.
- Play is not frivolous — it is often where truth and renewal arise.

Creativity is less about inventing from scratch and more about listening for what wants to emerge through you.

Practice: Creative Clearing

Set a timer for 20 minutes. Make two lists:

1. Projects, offerings, or practices that feel stale or draining.
2. Ideas, curiosities, or experiments you have been ignoring.

Choose one item from list one to end or pause, and one item from list two to give a small dose of attention. Notice how it shifts your energy.

Reflection Questions

- Where has my creativity gone dormant?
- What new ideas are waiting for space?
- What could end to create room for the next expression?

CHAPTER 17:
Resilience

Resilience is the capacity to bend without breaking, to adapt without losing center, and to rise again when circumstances change. It is not about never falling — it is about learning how to meet endings, disruptions, and disappointments with presence and renewal.

Resilience Beyond Endurance

Resilience is often mistaken for toughness or grit — the ability to push through no matter what. But pushing past limits is not resilience; it is survival mode. True resilience allows you to pause, to recalibrate, to learn, and even to end gracefully when that is what integrity requires.

Resilience is not resistance to change. It is the wisdom to move with change, trusting that every ending carries the seed of a new beginning.

Real-World Reflection

Dev, an entrepreneur, poured a year into a product launch that flopped. At first, he felt crushed — ashamed, fearful, and ready to give up. But as he reflected, he saw the launch differently. It had shown him what his audience truly needed, revealed where his systems were weak, and clarified what he no longer wished to carry forward.

Instead of labeling it a failure, he treated it as a teacher. He paused, integrated the lessons, and redesigned his business from a stronger foundation. His next offering was smaller but more aligned — and it succeeded. What once felt like collapse became the soil of resilience.

The field reminds us:

- Resilience grows through endings as much as through triumphs.

- Every disruption is feedback, not a verdict.

- Rising again doesn't always mean trying again — sometimes it means letting go with grace.

Resilience is not about avoiding difficulty but about walking with it until it transforms into wisdom.

Practice: The Gift in the Setback

Think of a recent disappointment or challenge in your business. Journal about it, then list three gifts it offered you:

- A lesson learned

- A clarity gained

- A burden released

Ask yourself: Does resilience here mean trying again with new wisdom, or ending this path so another can open?

Reflection Questions

- What has tested my resilience recently?

- What have I learned through loss or disruption?

- Where is resilience calling me to release, not push forward?

CHAPTER 18:
Expansion

Expansion is natural — but it is not permanent. Every growth is followed by integration, contraction, and rest. Expansion without pause collapses into exhaustion. Sustainable expansion requires rhythm, alignment, and discernment.

The Illusion of Endless Growth

Business culture often glorifies constant upward motion: more sales, more visibility, more offers, more everything. But nature reminds us that expansion always cycles back to stillness. The inhale is followed by the exhale. The bloom is followed by compost.

To expand well is to know your edges. Expansion rooted in alignment feels spacious; expansion driven by pressure feels frantic. The difference is not in the size of growth, but in its source.

Real-World Reflection

Sofia, a wellness entrepreneur, doubled her offerings in a single year. Revenue grew, but so did her overwhelm. She felt scattered, depleted, and increasingly disconnected from her original mission.

Her turning point came when she paused to review her growth. She identified which offerings nourished her, which drained her, and which were ready to end. By pruning and simplifying, she made room for sustainable expansion — growth that supported her life rather than consumed it. Her revenue steadied, but more importantly, her joy returned.

The field reminds us:

- Expansion is cyclical — inhale and exhale, bloom and rest.
- True expansion is balanced by integration.
- Endings are part of growth — pruning creates room for new vitality.
- Expansion without contraction leads to burnout; contraction without expansion leads to stagnation.
- Both are needed.

Practice: The Quarterly Review of Growth

At the end of each quarter, map your work into three categories:

- Scale — What is ready to grow?
- Sustain — What is steady and needs care, not change?
- Release — What is complete and can be ended with gratitude?

This practice prevents expansion from scattering your energy and keeps growth aligned with truth.

Reflection Questions

- Where is expansion alive in me now?
- Where am I overextending?
- What must end so that true expansion can last?

CHAPTER 19:
Stewardship

Stewardship is leadership rooted in care. It is the willingness to tend what has been entrusted to you — people, resources, vision, and even endings — with integrity. To steward is to remember that a business is not only something you own, but something you care for.

Beyond Ownership

Traditional models of leadership focus on control and possession: my company, my team, my results. Stewardship shifts the lens. It asks: how can I tend this work so it thrives for all it touches?

Sometimes stewardship means planting something new. Sometimes it means pruning what no longer fits. And sometimes, it means allowing a business to complete its cycle with dignity, so that the field of your life can be replenished.

Real World Reflection

Malik inherited his family's retail business. For years, he chased growth at all costs — adding new product lines, opening more locations, expanding faster than his systems could sustain. The business looked successful from the outside, but inside it was fragile, draining resources and joy.

When Malik embraced stewardship, he slowed down. He closed locations that were bleeding energy, simplified offerings to reflect the heart of the brand, and reconnected with longtime customers. Instead of trying to own everything, he began to tend what mattered. The business became smaller but healthier, more sustainable, and more aligned with its legacy.

The field reminds us:

- You are not an owner separate from the whole — you are a steward within it.

- Stewardship is care, not control.

- Sometimes the most faithful act of stewardship is to let something end, trusting that the soil will nourish what comes next.

Stewardship is not about size or speed. It is about integrity in how you hold what has been placed in your care.

Practice: Resource Inventory

Each quarter, take an honest inventory of your resources — financial, relational, and energetic. Ask:

- Where am I overspending or overextending?

- Where am I neglecting what matters most?

- What needs pruning or release so that true care can continue?

Let this practice shift you from ownership to guardianship — from grasping to tending.

Reflection Questions

- What has been entrusted to me?

- How am I tending it?

- What might stewardship mean in endings, not just in growth?

CHAPTER 20:
Presence

Presence is power. When you show up fully, people feel it. Presence cannot be faked — it requires you to be here, now. It is the quality that makes your leadership magnetic, not because you have all the answers, but because you are fully available to the moment.

The Cost of Distraction

In today's world, distraction is constant. Multitasking has become a badge of honor, but divided attention erodes trust and weakens connections. When your mind is scattered between emails, meetings, and plans, your presence fragments — and so does your leadership.

Presence asks you to slow down, to breathe, to give your full attention to the person or task in front of you. This is not inefficiency; it is devotion. Presence communicates value more clearly than any words.

Real-World Reflection

Rina, a team lead, noticed her staff growing increasingly disengaged. Meetings felt rushed, decisions unclear, morale low. She realized that while she was physically present, her attention was always divided — scanning emails, preparing for the next call, or worrying about deadlines.

She made a shift: closing her laptop in meetings, silencing notifications, and beginning each session with three deep breaths. Over time, her team responded. Trust deepened, conversations grew more honest, and projects flowed more smoothly. By offering her full attention, she restored the connection. Presence became her most powerful leadership tool.

The field reminds us:

- Presence is not performance; it is availability.
- To be fully here, you must release the need to control what comes next.
- Sometimes the most powerful presence is stillness — pausing long enough for truth to arise.

Presence does not demand more time; it demands more attention.

Practice: Three Breath Reset

Before your next meeting, client call, or creative session:

- Place your phone aside.
- Take three deep, conscious breaths.
- Set the intention: I am fully here for this moment.

Notice how even a brief reset shifts your energy — and the energy of the room.

Reflection Questions

- Where do I lose presence most easily?
- What practices restore me to here and now?
- How might presence guide me to pause or conclude with dignity?

CHAPTER 21:
Failure as Teacher

Failure is not the opposite of success — it is its companion. Every ending carries wisdom, every disappointment contains a lesson, every collapse clears space for renewal. When we shift our relationship with failure, we discover that it is less a verdict and more a teacher.

Redefining Failure

Culturally, we treat failure as shame, as evidence of inadequacy, as something to be hidden. Yet most breakthroughs are born from what didn't work first. Failure clarifies boundaries, reveals misalignment, and teaches discernment.

The pain of failure is real, but so is its gift. To let failure teach is to allow grief, reflection, and reorientation. To deny it is to repeat the same patterns, only louder.

Real-World Reflection

Adrian poured a year into developing a product launch that flopped. He invested resources, time, and his sense of identity into making it succeed. When sales fell short, shame rushed in. For weeks, he avoided looking at the numbers, terrified that they would confirm his worst fears.

Eventually, he sat with the data, not as punishment but as a teacher.

He realized the offer wasn't aligned with what his audience actually needed. More importantly, he recognized that he no longer wanted to carry that version of his business forward. The so-called failure freed him from a path that wasn't true. From its ashes, he built something more alive, more resonant, and more sustainable.

The field reminds us:

- Failure is feedback, not a final sentence.
- Endings disguised as failure are often thresholds into new beginnings.
- Gratitude for what "didn't work" turns failure into fuel.

When you honor failure as part of the cycle, it ceases to be an enemy. It becomes an ally in your becoming.

Practice: A Thank-You Letter to Failure

Think of a recent failure — a launch that fell flat, a project that didn't complete, a dream that didn't take root. Write a thank-you letter to it. Name the lessons it offered. Name the burdens it released. End the letter with gratitude for what this ending has made possible.

Reflection Questions

- What has failure taught me about myself as a leader?
- Where might a so-called failure actually be a release in disguise?
- What endings in my past became the soil for new beginnings?

CHAPTER 22:
Grief in Business

Grief is love with nowhere to go. It is part of business, though it is rarely named. We grieve the endings of dreams that never took root, the closing of a beloved venture, the loss of identity tied to work, or the slow fading of something that once felt alive.

The Hidden Presence of Grief

Most leaders are taught to hide grief — to treat it as weakness or irrelevance in the professional sphere. Yet grief is inevitable in business. Projects end. Clients leave. Teams dissolve. Markets shift.

To ignore grief is to numb yourself to the very love that gave rise to your work in the first place. To honor grief is to dignify your devotion, to remember that endings are as holy as beginnings.

Real-World Reflection

Priya, a café owner, poured years of care into her small shop. It became a hub for community, creativity, and connection. But rising rents and declining margins forced her to close. On the last day, she wept as she locked the door for the final time.

For weeks, she carried shame — believing she had failed. But over time, she created small rituals to honor what the café had given her. She lit candles for the friendshipsformed there, journaled about the lessons learned, and spoke gratitude for the years of service.

In naming her grief, she also named her love. The closure became less of a failure and more of a sacred completion.

The field reminds us:

- Grief is not an interruption — it is part of the cycle
- To grieve is to honor what was loved.
- When grief is welcomed, it clears space for joy to return.

Business is not separate from humanity. Where there is love, there will also be grief.

Practice: A Ritual for Release

Choose one loss in your business — an offer, a dream, a client, or even a whole company. Create a simple ritual to honor it:

- Light a candle.
- Write its name on paper.
- Speak gratitude for what it gave you.
- Release it — by tearing the paper, burning it, burying it, or placing it in water.

Let grief have its place. Let love be acknowledged.

Reflection Questions

- What grief am I carrying in my work?

- How might I honor it instead of rushing past it?

- What has grief taught me about the cycles of endings and beginnings?

CHAPTER 23:

Joy

Joy is not frivolous. It is fuel. It is what makes the work sustainable, luminous, and alive. Without joy, leadership becomes mechanical. With joy, leadership becomes magnetic.

Joy as Compass

Many of us treat joy as a reward for success — something to be earned after the launch, the milestone, the achievement. But joy is not the afterglow. It is the guide. When joy is present, it signals alignment. When joy disappears, it signals misalignment.

Joy doesn't always look like laughter or excitement. Sometimes it looks like peace, ease, or flow. To lead with joy is to trust that what lights you up also sustains those you serve.

Real-World Reflection

Sahana, a consultant, built her business for efficiency. Every process was optimized, every calendar block scheduled, every margin maximized. Yet something essential went missing — joy. She noticed herself dreading the very work she once loved.

Her shift came when she began letting joy back in. She released contracts that drained her, said yes to more playful collaborations, and carved out time for creative projectswith no agenda. The result wasn't only personal happiness — her clients noticed too. Her renewed vitality drew people closer, reminding them why they had trusted her in the first place.

The field reminds us:

- Joy is not indulgence — it is instruction.
- Joy clarifies what is true.
- Joy often waits on the other side of release.

When you follow joy, you move toward what is most alive. And when you honor endings that dim joy, you create space for joy to return.

Practice: The Joy Audit

Make three lists:

1. Joy-Filled — the tasks& relationships that light you up.
2. Joy-Neutral — the ones that are steady but not energizing.
3. Joy-Void — the ones that consistently drain you.

Commit to spending at least 10% more time each month in the Joy-Filled column. Choose one item from the Joy-Void list to delegate, simplify, or end.

Reflection Questions

- What brings me joy in my work?
- Where has joy gone missing?
- What can I complete so that joy has room to return?

CHAPTER 24:
Discernment

Discernment is the art of knowing which door to walk through — and which to close. It is clarity in action, the quiet wisdom that helps you choose fewer, truer paths instead of scattering your energy across every option.

The Gift of Fewer Yeses

Opportunities are constant in business: new collaborations, new platforms, new ideas, new clients. Without discernment, you risk chasing everything and completing nothing. The result is fragmentation, fatigue, and a sense of always being behind.

Discernment is not only about choosing what to pursue. It is equally about choosing what to release. Saying no with clarity is as sacred as saying yes with confidence.

Real World Reflection

Theo, a coach, found himself pulled in many directions — consulting opportunities, speaking invitations, online courses, and collaborations. Each one looked promising, but together they left him exhausted and unfocused.

Through discernment, he began filtering opportunities not by external appeal but by resonance. He asked: Does this align with my deepest values? Does this feel alive in my body? Does this opportunity

nourish or deplete me? By choosing fewer paths and closing the rest, Theo found renewed energy and greater impact. What once felt like a lack of direction became alignment through simplicity.

The field reminds us:

- Discernment is not about fear of missing out; it is about devotion to truth.

- Every no protects the integrity of your yes.

- Closure is clarity in motion.

Discernment brings peace because it narrows the field to what is truly yours to hold.

Practice: The Three-Door Exercise

Write down three opportunities or decisions you are currently considering. Imagine fully committing to each — not just the surface outcome, but the energy required to sustain it. Notice:

- Which feels expansive?

- Which feels heavy or misaligned?

- Which is rooted in fear, and which in truth?

Choose the door that feels alive. Close the rest with gratitude.

Reflection Questions

- Where do I struggle to choose?
- What am I afraid of ending?

CHAPTER 25:
Wholeness

Wholeness is integration — the weaving together of all your parts into a cohesive whole. It is the sense that nothing essential is missing, and nothing false is being carried forward. Wholeness does not come from adding more to yourself, but from releasing what fragments you.

Beyond Fragmentation

Many leaders unconsciously split themselves into parts: the professional self and the personal self, the visionary and the pragmatist, the spiritual seeker and the business builder. While compartmentalization may seem useful, over time it creates dissonance. What you hide takes energy to maintain.

Wholeness invites you to stop separating and start integrating. To let your soul and your strategy meet. To bring your full self into your leadership, even if it feels vulnerable.

Real-World Reflection

Imani, a consultant, kept her spirituality hidden from her business. She feared it would make her seem unprofessional. But the more she hid, the more drained she felt. intuitive nudges and naming her values openly.

Eventually, she began weaving spiritual practices into her work — opening meetings with breath, trusting Her clients didn't resist; they welcomed it. What had once felt like a liability became her unique strength. By integrating what she once exiled, she experienced wholeness — and her business became an authentic expression of her full self.

The field reminds us:

- Wholeness is not perfection — it is presence.
- What you exile fragments you; what you integrate restores you.
- To return to wholeness, something false often needs to end.

Wholeness is not about becoming more, but about becoming true.

Practice: The Circle of Life

Draw a circle and divide it into the key parts of your life: business, health, relationships, creativity, spirituality, and rest. Shade in how nourished each feels right now. Where is energy abundant? Where is energy leaking?

Ask: What needs to be released so that energy can flow back into balance?

Reflection Questions

- What parts of me are still exiled from my work?
- What would integration look like in my leadership?
- What might I need to end to return to wholeness?

CHAPTER 26:
Legacy

Legacy is not only what you achieve — it is what you leave behind. It is the imprint of your presence, the energy of your choices, and the ripple of your work in the lives of others. Legacy is not a distant concept for the end of your career; it is being shaped in every decision you make now.

Beyond Achievement

In the business world, legacy is often equated with awards, accolades, or institutions that endure. But true legacy is more intimate. It is the way you treat people, the energy you bring into spaces, and the wisdom you pass on through your work.

Legacy is shaped not just by what you start, but by what you complete. Sometimes the most powerful mark you leave is knowing when to step aside, allowing others to rise.

Real World Reflection

Asha, a mentor to emerging leaders, once believed her legacy would be measured in milestones — programs built, revenue earned, recognition gained. But as the years passed, she realized her true legacy was not the projects themselves but the people she had lifted. The colleagues she encouraged, the students she mentored, the clients she empowered. Part of her legacy also came from endings — knowing when to close an offer that had run its course, when to pass leadership to someone else, when to let her voice quiet so another could be heard. By releasing control, she allowed her legacy to be not just what she created, but what she made space for others to create.

The field reminds us:

- Legacy is not built in a single act — it is woven daily

- Endings shape legacy as much as beginnings.

- Your true legacy is how people feel in your presence and what continues through them after you are gone.

Legacy is alive. It is less about what you hold on to and more about what you entrust to others.

Practice: Writing Your Business Eulogy

Write a eulogy for your business as if it were complete today. What would you want it to be remembered for? Who would you want it to have touched? What values would you want to echo through its work?

Then ask: What needs to end now to protect that legacy? What needs to continue to strengthen it?

Reflection Questions

- What legacy am I shaping through my daily choices?

- What do I want to be remembered for?

- What completions might actually protect or strengthen my legacy?

CHAPTER 27:
Light Leads

Leadership is not domination — it is illumination. To lead with light is to shine clearly enough that others can see their own way forward. Sometimes that light reveals the path of growth, sometimes the pause of integration, and sometimes the sacred threshold of completion.

Illumination Over Control

Traditional models of leadership often equate strength with certainty, authority with control. But light does not force. Light reveals. When you lead with light, you don't have to have all the answers — you have to be willing to hold space for truth, even if it disrupts the plan.

Light-led leadership honors cycles. It knows that guiding someone toward an ending can be as powerful as guiding them toward a beginning.

Real-World Reflection

Niko, a mentor for emerging leaders, once believed leadership meant always knowing the way forward. He worked tirelessly to project confidence, to offer solutions, to carry the weight of others' uncertainty. But over time, this performance drained him and left his students dependent rather than empowered.

When Niko began leading with light, his approach shifted. Instead of always giving directions, he asked questions. Instead of fixing, he illuminated choices. Instead of pushing his mentees forward, he honored their rhythms — including when one chose to leave the program because their path had been completed. Paradoxically, by letting go of control, his influence deepened. His students began to trust themselves, not just him.

The field reminds us:

- Light leads without coercion.

- Illumination reveals both beginnings and completions

- Leadership is less about knowing the way and more about holding the lantern steady.

To lead with light is to trust that truth, once illuminated, is enough.

Practice: The Lantern Question

In your next decision or conversation, instead of asking, what will make me look strong? Ask, what will shed the most light here?

Sometimes that light will guide you forward. Sometimes it will reveal the need for a pause. And sometimes it will clarify that a chapter is complete.

Reflection Questions

- How do I currently define leadership?

- Where am I asked to illuminate rather than control?

- How might light lead me to honor a completion?

CHAPTER 28:
Crossing the Sacred Threshold

The Art of Ending Well

Every cycle carries its own completion. The seed becomes the flower, the flower becomes the fruit, and the fruit falls back to the soil. Endings are not failures; they are thresholds. To end well is to honor the wisdom of the cycle, to release with grace what has run its course, and to trust that new life will emerge in time.

The Shame Around Endings

In business, endings are often hidden. We quietly close programs, dissolve partnerships, or walk away from ventures while pretending nothing has changed. This silence is born from shame — the belief that ending equals failure.

But endings are not failures. They are teachers. They are thresholds of transformation. To end well is to restore dignity to yourself, your work, and those who walked with you along the way.

Real World Reflection

I know this threshold intimately. After decades of devotion to a business I poured my soul into, I found myself facing potential bankruptcy. The word itself felt like a scarlet letter stamped on my efforts. I believed for a time that if I just worked harder, offered more, or led with greater heart, things would turn around.

But the numbers told another truth. Debt mounted. Joy eroded. Exhaustion deepened. Eventually, I sat in my lawyer's office, both devastated and strangely free. In that moment, I realized this ending was not a mark of failure but a rite of passage. It stripped away illusions of control and invited me into humility, discernment, and the deeper wisdom of completion.

What I once resisted has become my teacher. It showed me that endings are holy ground. They are not the end of the story, but the fertile soil for what comes next.

The field reminds us:

- Endings are sacred thresholds, not verdicts.

- Completion is not loss; it is integration.

- When you honor endings with ritual, gratitude, and truth, they become blessings.

To cross the threshold with light is to carry forward the gifts, release the burdens, and trust that even in loss, life is quietly renewing itself.

Practices for Sacred Release

- Closure Inventory — List everything this business or season gave you: skills, relationships, wisdom, resilience. Honor each one.

- Gratitude Ritual — Light a candle and read your list aloud. Speak thanks as if addressing a beloved teacher.

- Release Ceremony — Burn or shred symbolic items (old contracts, notes, to-do lists) as an act of letting go.

- Debt Forgiveness — For every financial or emotional debt, pair it with an affirmation of forgiveness — for yourself, for the system, for the story.

- Mark the Threshold — Choose a date to declare closure. Cross it with intention — through a walk, a prayer, or sharing the truth with your community.

Reflection Questions

- What am I carrying forward from this season?

- What am I ready to release completely?

- How can I honor my business not as a failure, but as a teacher?

- What ritual would help me mark this threshold?

This book is not a straight path but a spiral. Each chapter offers a facet of leadership, but together they form a rhythm: vision, alignment, growth, pause, and completion. To lead from light is to honor all seasons, not just the ones that look shiny from the outside.

Embracing the Full Arc

Most of us have been conditioned to celebrate beginnings — the launch, the new client, the bold idea. But light-led leadership dignifies every stage: the seed, the bloom, the harvest, and the return to soil. Expansion and contraction, creation and release, joy and grief — all are part of the same holy cycle.

The field of your business is alive. Like any living thing, it requires nourishment, rest, pruning, and renewal. Ignoring this truth leads to burnout. Honoring it leads to wisdom.

Practical Integration

As you carry these teachings forward, consider these practices to live the cycles in your work:

- Build pauses into your calendar — treat rest and reflection with the same weight as launches and deadlines.

- Mark completions with ritual — close projects and businesses with gratitude, not silence.

- Honor grief in business — allow yourself and your team to name loss as part of the journey.

- Let endings teach you — reflect on what is complete before rushing into what is next.

A LEADER OF LIGHT

To be a leader of light is not to avoid difficulty, but to walk through it with presence. It is to illuminate, not control. To remember that what begins will one day end, and that what ends will nourish what comes next.

Your leadership will be remembered not because you never faltered, but because you honored the full spiral of becoming.

A Final Blessing

May you lead with clarity when it is time to build.
May you rest with trust when it is time to pause.
May you release with grace when it is time to end.
And through it all, may you remember:
Light leads. Always.

ABOUT THE AUTHOR

With 25 years of experience across the peaks and valleys of
entrepreneurship — including running a multi-million-dollar creative
agency through the uncharted waters of COVID, cancer, and the
devastating loss of a child — Melita Callahan writes from both the
boardroom and the soul. She knows firsthand that leadership isn't
just about scaling revenue; it's about holding vision when the lights
flicker, finding devotion when energy runs low, and learning when to
courageously let go.

Rooted in Portland, Oregon, where she lives with her husband and their
dog (who is sure he's the true CEO), she balances business strategy
with a love for kayaking the rivers and riding motorcycles on winding
country roads. Her work is infused with conscious leadership, mystical
light, and the kind of practical wisdom you can apply to quarterly
planning — or to navigating the wild adventure of inbox zero.

Light Leads reflects her belief that strategy can be soulful, endings
can be holy, and that sometimes the most powerful leadership move is
to pause, breathe, and listen for the unseen currents of guidance. She
writes not as someone who has avoided hardship, but as someone who
has walked through it and still chooses to lead with light — and maybe
a little laughter along the way.

Continue Walking in the Field of Light

The journey doesn't end here. If *Light Leads* has spoken to something deep within you, you're invited to explore further through the **Field of Light Oracle Deck** and **channeled writings** from the **Council of Light** at Nova-Asha.com.

These transmissions are companions for the path—each one an invitation to listen more closely, to remember your luminous origins, and to live and lead from the light that never leaves you.

Welcome home to the Field. You've always belonged here.

APPENDIX

Practice: The Living Manifesto

Write a one-page manifesto for your business as if it were a living being. Ask:

- What does it stand for?

- What season is it in - growth, pause, or completion?

- What is it asking you to release?

Practice: The Alignment Audit

Take out your weekly calendar. Map your activities against your deepest values.

- Circle what feels alive, nourishing, and true.

- Cross out what feels draining, heavy, or false.

For the places of dissonance, ask: Does this need a shift, a pause, or a completion?

Treat this as a living ritual, not a one-time exercise. Alignment is dynamic; it asks for ongoing attention.

Practice: The Voice of Authority

Record yourself speaking about your work for three minutes without notes. Then listen back:

- Note the words and phrases that feel alive, authentic, and magnetic.

  - Notice where your energy drops — these are places that may be misaligned or asking to be released.

This practice reveals the difference between what you perform and what you embody.

Practice: The Timing Triage

Each month, list three opportunities, projects, or decisions you feel pressure to pursue. Then:

- Circle the one that feels ripe now.

- Cross out the one that feels premature or forced.

- Place the third on a "someday" list to revisit later.

This practice helps you discern between urgency and true readiness.

Practice: The Devotional No

For one week, track every request that comes your way — emails, collaborations, invitations, even internal impulses. Each day, choose at least one thing to decline, gently but firmly.

Notice how your body responds. Do you feel lighter, clearer, more spacious? Let each no become a practice of devotion — to your work, your energy, and your truth.

Practice: Letters of Love and Release

Write a love letter to your work — naming what you cherish, what still lights you up, and what you feel called to sustain.

Then, write a farewell letter to any part of your business that no longer aligns. Thank it for what it gave you and release it with grace.

Both letters are acts of devotion. One honors what you are carrying forward; the other dignifies what is complete.

Practice: Cycle Mapping

Draw a simple wheel of the year, divided into four seasons. Place your launches on this wheel. Then, mark:

- Which season is for planting (visioning, pre-launch groundwork)?

- Which is for blossoming (the active launch)?

- Which is for harvest (serving, delivering, receiving the fruits)?

- Which is for rest (integration, reflection, renewal)?

Notice: Are you honoring each phase, or skipping straight from planting to planting, never allowing the soil to restore?

Practice: The Integrity Inventory

Write a list of all your current commitments — clients, projects, collaborations, and internal goals. For each, ask:

- Does this still feel true?

- Does this reflect my deepest values?

- If not, what would integrity call me to do — pause, shift, or complete?

Let this audit become a regular rhythm. Each realignment restores wholeness.

Practice: Naming the Fear, Honoring the Truth

Each week, name one thing you are afraid to admit about your business or leadership. Please write it down. Share it, if you can, with a trusted peer or mentor.

Then ask:

- What truth is this fear protecting?

- What would courage look like here — to act, to wait, or to end?

By naming fear and uncovering the truth beneath it, you invite courage to walk with you.

Practice: Rhythms of Renewal

Schedule three kinds of rest into your life and business:

- Daily pauses — short breaks that reset your energy.

- Weekly renewal — longer moments of restoration, like a day of rest, nature walks, or play.

- Seasonal retreats — intentional times of stepping away from your business to listen, restore, and reconnect.

Protect these spaces as fiercely as you protect deadlines. They are not luxuries — they are leadership practices. Make a list of rests you have gifted yourself this year and reflect on what they have given back to you.

Practice: The One-Question Silence

In your next conversation — with a client, a colleague, or yourself — ask a single open-ended question. Then remain silent for at least one full minute. Resist the urge to fill the space. Notice what arises.

This practice cultivates patience, presence, and trust that wisdom does not need to be forced — it will surface in its own time.

Practice: The Boundary Audit

This month, choose one area of your business to bring into alignment. Ask:

- Where do I feel resentment building?

- Where am I giving more than I wish to give?

- What boundary would restore devotion here?

Then set one new boundary — whether it's response times, meeting limits, or project scope. Communicate it clearly and honor it consistently.

Practice: The Trust Ledger

Create a journal or document where you list evidence of trust in your business. Record moments when:

- A client came easily without forcing.

- A pivot worked even when logic doubted it.

- A synchronicity opened doors. A promise was honored, even in difficulty.

When doubt creeps in, return to this ledger. Let it remind you that trust has already carried you this far — and will continue to do so.

Practice: Power Reclaimed

List three areas in your business or leadership where you feel most drained. For each, ask:

- What truth have I been avoiding here?

- What decision would release energy back to me?

- Is it time to act, to delegate, or to end?

Choose one small but powerful action this week — not to prove your strength, but to align your energy.

Practice: Three Honest Shares

Reach out to three peers, colleagues, or members of your circle. Share one honest update with each — not just successes, but struggles.

Notice who can hold you with care. Let this become a doorway into deeper belonging.

Practice: Creative Clearing

Set a timer for 20 minutes. Make two lists:

1. Projects, offerings, or practices that feel stale or draining.

2. Ideas, curiosities, or experiments you have been ignoring.

Choose one item from list one to end or pause, and one item from list two to give a small dose of attention. Notice how it shifts your energy.

Practice: The Gift in the Setback

Think of a recent disappointment or challenge in your business. Journal about it, then list three gifts it offered you:

- A lesson learned

- A clarity gained

- A burden released

Ask yourself: Does resilience here mean trying again with new wisdom, or ending this path so another can open?

Practice: The Quarterly Review of Growth

At the end of each quarter, map your work into three categories:

- Scale — What is ready to grow?

- Sustain — What is steady and needs care, not change?

- Release — What is complete and can be ended with gratitude?

This practice prevents expansion from scattering your energy and keeps growth aligned with truth.

Practice: Resource Inventory

Each quarter, take an honest inventory of your resources — financial, relational, and energetic. Ask:

- Where am I overspending or overextending?

- Where am I neglecting what matters most?

- What needs pruning or release so that true care can continue?

Let this practice shift you from ownership to guardianship — from grasping to tending.

Practice: Three-Breath Reset

Before your next meeting, client call, or creative session:

- Place your phone aside.

- Take three deep, conscious breaths.

- Set the intention: I am fully here for this moment.

Notice how even a brief reset shifts your energy — and the energy of the room.

Practice: A Thank You Letter to Failure

Think of a recent failure — a launch that fell flat, a project that didn't complete, a dream that didn't take root. Write a thank-you letter to it. Name the lessons it offered. Name the burdens it released. End the letter with gratitude for what this ending has made possible.

Practice: A Ritual for Release

Choose one loss in your business — an offer, a dream, a client, or even a whole company. Create a simple ritual to honor it:

- Light a candle.

- Write its name on paper.

- Speak gratitude for what it gave you.

- Release it — by tearing the paper, burning it, burying it, or placing it in water.

Let grief have its place. Let love be acknowledged.

Practice: The Joy Audit

Make three lists:

1. Joy-Filled — the tasks& relationships that light you up.

2. Joy-Neutral — the ones that are steady but not energizing.

3. Joy-Void — the ones that consistently drain you.

Commit to spending at least 10% more time each month in the Joy-Filled column. Choose one item from the Joy-Void list to delegate, simplify, or end.

Practice: The Three-Door Exercise

Write down three opportunities or decisions you are currently considering. Imagine fully committing to each — not just the surface outcome, but the energy required to sustain it. Notice:

- Which feels expansive?

- Which feels heavy or misaligned?

- Which is rooted in fear, and which in truth?

Choose the door that feels alive. Close the rest with gratitude.

Practice: The Circle of Life

Draw a circle and divide it into the key parts of your life: business, health, relationships, creativity, spirituality, and rest. Shade in how nourished each feels right now. Where is energy abundant? Where is energy leaking?

Ask: What needs to be released so that energy can flow back into balance?

Practice: Writing Your Business Eulogy

Write a eulogy for your business as if it were complete today. What would you want it to be remembered for? Who would you want it to have touched? What values would you want to echo through its work?

Then ask: What needs to end now to protect that legacy? What needs to continue to strengthen it?

Practice: The Lantern Question

In your next decision or conversation, instead of asking, what will make me look strong? Ask, what will shed the most light here?

Sometimes that light will guide you forward. Sometimes it will reveal the need for a pause. And sometimes it will clarify that a chapter is complete.

Practices for Sacred Release

- Closure Inventory — List everything this business or season gave you: skills, relationships, wisdom, resilience. Honor each one

- Gratitude Ritual — Light a candle and read your list aloud. Speak thanks as if addressing a beloved teacher.

- Release Ceremony — Burn or shred symbolic items (old contracts, notes, to-do lists) as an act of letting go.

- Debt Forgiveness — For every financial or emotional debt, pair it with an affirmation of forgiveness — for yourself, for the system, for the story.

- Mark the Threshold — Choose a date to declare closure. Cross it with intention — through a walk, a prayer, or sharing the truth with your community.

The Field of Vision Reflection Questions

- What is my vision asking of me now?

- Where is my vision misaligned with my current offerings?

- What part of my vision might be complete — making space for what wants to be born?

Alignment Reflection Questions

- Where in my business am I out of alignment?

- What am I doing only because I think I "should"?

- What would alignment look like if I honored endings as much as beginnings?

Authority Reflection Questions

- What gives me the deepest sense of authority in my work?

- Where am I performing authority instead of embodying it?

- What would it look like to end something that undermines my authority?

Timing Reflection Questions

- What am I trying to force before it's season?

- What is ripe and ready now?

- What is asking to be delayed, or even completed?

The Sacred No Reflection Questions

- Where am I called to say no right now?

- What ends when I decline, and what space opens up?

- How could a "no" be an act of completion rather than resistance?

Devotion Reflection Questions

- What am I most devoted to now?

- Where has devotion turned into exhaustion?

- What would devotion look like if I honored rest and endings as much as beginnings?

Rhythm of Launches Reflection Questions

- What is my natural rhythm of creating and resting?

- Which offerings are ready for another launch, and which are complete?

- How can I honor the fallow season as much as the harvest?

Integrity Reflection Questions

- Where am I living in integrity?

- Where have I drifted from what I most value?

- What commitments might need to be released to restore wholeness?

Courage Reflection Questions

- Where is fear holding me back from the truth?

- What action would courage take now?

- What would it mean to complete something courageously?

Rest Reflection Questions

- What kind of rest do I resist most?

- Where does my business need a pause?

- What might need to end so that true rest is possible?

Listening Reflection Questions

- Where am I avoiding listening because it feels uncomfortable?

- What is my business asking me to hear right now?

- What pauses or completions are being whispered to me that I ignore?

Boundaries as Devotion Reflection Questions

- Where does my lack of boundaries erode my devotion?
- What new boundary would nourish me most?
- What might need to end if I am to stay true to myself?

Trust Reflection Questions

- Where am I tempted to exaggerate or overcommit?

- What does trustworthy leadership look like for me right now?

- Where might trust be strengthened by closure instead of continuation?

Power Reflection Questions

- Where am I giving away my power?

- How does aligned power want to move through me now?

- Where might the most powerful act be to stop, rather than to continue?

- What decision would release energy back to me?

Community Reflection Questions

- Where am I isolating instead of leaning into community?

- What support am I resisting?

- Who could help me honor a pause or an ending with dignity?

Creativity Reflection Questions

- Where has my creativity gone dormant?

- What new ideas are waiting for space?

- What could end to create room for the next expression?

Resilience Reflection Questions

- What has tested my resilience recently?

- What have I learned through loss or disruption?

- Where is resilience calling me to release, not push forward?

Expansion Reflection Questions

- Where is expansion alive in me now?

- Where am I overextending?

- What must end so that true expansion can last?

Stewardship Reflection Questions

- What has been entrusted to me?

- How am I tending it?

- What might stewardship mean in endings, not just in growth?

Presence Reflection Questions

- Where do I lose presence most easily?

- What practices restore me to here and now?

- How might presence guide me to pause or conclude with dignity?

Failure as a Teacher Reflection Questions

- What has failure taught me about myself as a leader?

- Where might a so-called failure actually be a release in disguise?

- What endings in my past became the soil for new beginnings?

Grief in Business Reflection Questions

- What grief am I carrying in my work?

- How might I honor it instead of rushing past it?

- What has grief taught me about the cycles of endings and beginnings?

Joy Reflection Questions

- What brings me joy in my work?

- Where has joy gone missing?

- What can I complete so that joy has room to return?

Discernment Reflection Questions

- Where do I struggle to choose?

- What am I afraid of ending?

Wholeness Reflection Questions

- What parts of me are still exiled from my work?

- What would integration look like in my leadership?

- What might I need to end to return to wholeness?

Legacy Reflection Questions

- What legacy am I shaping through my daily choices?

- What do I want to be remembered for?

- What completions might actually protect or strengthen my legacy?

Light Leads Reflection Questions

- How do I currently define leadership?

- Where am I asked to illuminate rather than control?

- How might light lead me to honor a completion?

Crossing the Sacred Threshold Reflection Questions

- What am I carrying forward from this season?

- What am I ready to release completely?

- How can I honor my business not as a failure, but as a teacher?

- What ritual would help me mark this threshold?